Offshore Sea Life ID Guide
East Coast

Steve N. G. Howell
Brian L. Sullivan

In collaboration with
Melanie White
Tom Johnson
and Brian Patteson

D0106886

Princeton University Press   Princeton and Oxford

An unusually curious Loggerhead Turtle.

Published by Princeton University Press, 41 William Street, Princeton, New Jersey 08540
In the United Kingdom: Princeton University Press, 6 Oxford Street, Woodstock, Oxfordshire OX20 1TW
press.princeton.edu

Cover image composite: Atlantic Puffin, White-tailed Tropicbird, Humpback Whale,
Atlantic White-sided Dolphin, Black-capped Petrel, and Sargassum Midget
© Brian L. Sullivan, Steve N. G. Howell, and Melanie White

Library of Congress Control Number: 2015939778
ISBN 978-0-691-16621-6 (pbk.)

British Library Cataloguing-in-Publication Data is available
This book has been composed in Minion Pro and Calibri
Printed on acid-free paper.
Printed in China
10 9 8 7 6 5 4 3 2 1

Offshore Sea Life ID Guide East Coast

Contents

Believed extinct by the 1600s, Bermuda Petrel (above) was rediscovered in the 1900s and its nesting grounds were located in 1951. This attractive gadfly petrel has since been the subject of an intensive conservation campaign, and today it is likely that 500 or so birds range over the North Atlantic. Still, the chances of seeing one off the East Coast remain slim.

Abbreviations. To save space we often use four-letter codes for species names; the codes are listed as an index on pp. 63–64. Likewise, standard state abbreviations are used: DE for Delaware, FL Florida, MA Massachusetts, MD Maryland, ME Maine, NC North Carolina, NH New Hampshire, NJ New Jersey, VA Virginia. For months we use 3 letters: Feb for February, Jun for June, etc. North, central, south, etc., are usually abbreviated as n., cen., s., etc. We use the Latin abbreviation 'cf.' for 'compare with.'

We define the Northeast as the Gulf of Maine south to Cape Cod, Massachusetts; the Mid-Atlantic Coast as Long Island, New York, south to Cape Hatteras, North Carolina; and the Southeast as Cape Hatteras south to Florida.

Introduction

What do the following have in common? Humpback Whales lunge-feeding and breaching, snappy-looking Black-capped Petrels wheeling over cobalt blue waters, multicolored flyingfish gliding over glassy seas flecked with golden Sargassum weed. Well, for the most part, you can't see them from shore. You'll need to experience these offshore wonders on a boat trip, often called a 'pelagic trip' by birdwatchers.

This identification guide uses plates of composite photos to help you identify offshore marine wildlife—'things you see at sea,' be they whales, birds, dolphins, turtles, sharks, or flyingfish. Short accounts distill the essence of identification—wildlife views at sea can be brief, and the less time you spend reading a book the better. Once you have a name, numerous other resources are available to help you learn more about the creatures that inhabit the oceans. But that all-important handle, a species name, is the first step in the cascade of knowledge.

We focus on species seen on day trips off the East Coast (Maine to central Florida; see map inside back cover), not those found far offshore in waters few people get to visit. Some species we include can be seen from shore but are also found offshore, and are usually considered as marine creatures. We don't include coastal birds such as most gulls, terns, cormorants, sea ducks, loons, grebes, or even some 'marine' mammals (they're called *Harbor* Seals for a reason; below); even though you may see these from boats they can all be watched more easily from shore. We also do not include real rarities, species you might never see even on 100 trips, such as a Bermuda Petrel (opposite).

Gray Seals (the 2 larger, longer-nosed animals near front) and Harbor Seals are inshore and coastal animals, seen on rocky headlands and islands, not truly offshore creatures.

The harder you look at the ocean the more you see. We cut off our coverage at about apple-size organisms, which is what most people are likely to notice. However, if you look carefully, on calm days you might see many more things, including the amazing sea skaters, ocean-going wingless insects related to the water striders you can see on freshwater ponds. Most species, like those shown below, occur in the Pacific Ocean, but one species, *Halobates micans*, can be seen off the Southeast. All species look very similar except under a microscope.

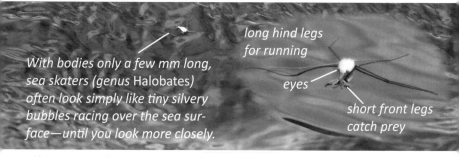

long hind legs for running

With bodies only a few mm long, sea skaters (genus *Halobates*) often look simply like tiny silvery bubbles racing over the sea surface—until you look more closely.

eyes

short front legs catch prey

One thing you'll soon notice is that wildlife is not evenly distributed at sea. On your way offshore you pass through the inshore zone, often alive with coastal 'seabirds' such as gulls, terns, pelicans, and cormorants, most of which tend to disappear when you get a few miles offshore. Then you are in the world of whales, petrels, and flyingfish—the pelagic zone.

Sargassum (below, and p. 60) often bunches up at fronts within the Gulf Stream. Such weedlines are good places to find terns, phalaropes, and flyingfish.

Although the ocean often looks much the same from a boat, it comprises different habitats, much as land does—but on land we can more easily see the difference between a field and a forest. Moreover, the habitats at sea are mobile, shifting with the currents and the wind. This means that it can be difficult to predict where whales or birds will be from day to day, as they track their food resources across a seemingly featureless ocean.

Luckily, food tends to be concentrated in certain areas because of predictable marine processes. The food web starts with plankton, tiny organisms that fuel themselves with sunlight and nutrients, like plants on land. Sunlight is easy to find anywhere near the surface, but most of the nutrients in the ocean have sunk to the deep over countless ages. A process known as upwelling can bring nutrients up into reach of the sunlight, and thus set in motion the cycle of life. For example, areas where two water masses meet, known as 'fronts,' can mix the water to generate upwelling and thus productivity.

Upwelling also occurs in places where currents run into topographic features of the seabed, such as canyon walls or mountains (often known

Few ocean fronts in the world are as stark as this mid-winter break between the cold green Labrador Current (at back, around 40°F) and the warm blue Gulf Stream (in front, around 60°F and warming rapidly away from the front). Food items, and thus birds (such as these Dovekies), often concentrate along such fronts. On another day, this exact same 'place' on the Earth's surface might look like the picture opposite, a vivid testament to the shifting nature of marine habitats.

as 'banks' when they are high enough to approach the surface). The underwater ridges and mountains north of Cape Cod, Massachusetts, known as Stellwagen Bank and Jeffreys Ledge, along with Georges Bank farther offshore, promote upwelling and help make the Gulf of Maine region such a hotspot for marine life.

Another important upwelling region, where underwater currents run into topography, is where the continental shelf drops off to the deep. The shelf is the relatively shallow seabed that extends from a continental landmass. The point at which it ends and the seabed drops off steeply is known as the 'shelf break.' Unlike along the West Coast, the continental shelf in the East is wide. It is not easy to reach the shelf break in a day trip other than off Cape Hatteras, North Carolina, helping explain why this is such a popular destination for birders.

Feeding swarms of Northern Gannets (below) are typical of cooler 'green waters' off the Northeast and, in winter, the Mid-Atlantic states.

While the productive 'green waters' off the Northeast support many whales and seabirds, the warm 'blue waters' of the Gulf Stream are relatively poor in life—the equivalent of deserts on land. But, as with land deserts, the blue waters have species adapted to that habitat, creatures not found in the cooler waters—such as tropicbirds and flyingfish.

Although offshore wildlife includes spectacular animals such as whales and gadfly petrels, as well as some birds in great abundance, the total number of species is manageable. In the region this guide covers, we consider only about 15 mammals and 35 bird species as regularly occurring offshore marine creatures likely to be seen on day trips. To balance this modest number, however, many of the species look quite similar, and viewing wildlife from a moving platform can be a challenge.

Medications can help with seasickness (if taken ahead of time), but many people do just fine on boats if they stay outside with the breeze in their face and a view of the horizon (don't sit in the cabin and read!). The ocean has only a finite range of motions, and observing swell direction and moving your body accordingly is a good idea—learn to move with the ocean, not fight against it.

Even when it's sunny and hot onshore it can be cool offshore on a boat, and it's better to bring extra clothes and not need them than to spend the day cold and uncomfortable. On summer trips remember to take lots of liquids and stay hydrated, as it can be really hot and sunny, at least from the Mid-Atlantic Coast southward. And don't forget your sunscreen, sunglasses, and a hat.

In warmer 'blue waters' off the Southeast, False Killer Whales (below) occasionally come in and bow-ride, putting on quite a show.

Obviously, bow-riding dolphins are best seen while the boat is moving, but otherwise the best and easiest viewing is often when the boat is stopped, either because whales have been spotted or because birds are coming in to feed on 'chum' (food thrown out behind the boat). Most wildlife can be appreciated simply with the naked eye, but binoculars are helpful when looking for smaller birds such as storm-petrels and phalaropes.

Now all that remains is to get out there and experience the magic of the open ocean. Enjoy!

Bow-riding Atlantic Spotted Dolphins

The long white pectoral flippers of this curious Hump-back Whale are here shown off well to its appreciative audience.

Acknowledgments

In 50 or so years of combined experience going out on boats to look for sea life we have met many who share our passion. We particularly thank Brian Patteson, Kate Sutherland, Ned Brinkley, and Dave Shoch. Others who helped include Louis Bevier, Michael Brothers, Nate Dias, Megan Elrod, Marshall Iliff, Dennis Jongsomjit, Derek Lovitch, Todd Mc-Grath, Sea McKeon, and Blair Nikula. Most photos used here are our own, but we thank collaborators Melanie White of Granite State Whale Watch, Brian Patteson of Seabirding Inc., and Tom Johnson, along with Michael Andersen, Robin W. Baird (www.cascadiaresearch.org), Daniel Behm, Nick Bonomo, Michael Brothers, Nate Dias, Bob Fogg, Yann Kolbeinsson, Larry Manfredi, Todd McGrath, Greg Morgan (www.gregmorganphotography. co.uk), Chris Sloan, and Jeremiah Trimble, for sharing their images.

Books offering additional information about East Coast sea life include *Whales, Dolphins, and Other Marine Mammals of the World* by H. Shirihai and B. Jarrett (2006), *Petrels, Albatrosses, and Storm-Petrels of North America* by S. N. G. Howell (2012), *A Field Guide to Coastal Fishes from Maine to Texas* by V. Kells and K. Carpenter, and *The Amazing World of Flyingfish* by S. N. G. Howell (2014).

Some Words Explained

Alcid (pronounced 'al-sid'): Any member of the auk family, including murres, Razorbill, puffins, guillemots, and Dovekie.

Blow: The spray blown skyward by a breathing whale.

Breaching: To leap clear or almost clear of the water.

Falcate: Having a curved, sickle-like shape.

Fluking: Raising of tail flukes above the surface as a whale dives.

Footprint: Slick area of water displaced at the surface when a whale or other marine creature sounds.

Logging: To lie at the sea surface, looking like a floating log.

Pelagic: Relating to the open ocean.

Porpoising: A mode of fast travel used mainly by dolphins, involving repeated low-angle leaps from the water.

Sounding: The action of a marine mammal diving to stay down for a while and usually leaving a 'footprint' at the surface.

Spy-hopping: To raise the head straight up out of the water, apparently to look around above the surface.

Tubenose: Any bird in the order Procellariiformes, which have nostrils housed in tubes on the bill, including shearwaters, petrels, and storm-petrels.

Marine Mammals

Unlike seabirds, marine mammals spend most of their time underwater, coming to the surface to breathe, and rarely do you see the whole animal. Views can be brief, and we provide the clues needed to identify species based on what you are likely to see—a fin, a blow, a tail going down.

As with 'seabirds,' some 'marine mammals' live along the coast, such as Harbor Seals and Gray Seals (see p. 5). We do not treat these species because they're not really offshore creatures; they can be seen more easily from land. Other marine mammals can be seen from shore on occasion, although to see them up close you'll still want to go out on a boat.

Things to look for with whales and dolphins are group size, general behavior, dorsal fin size and shape, any patterns or markings, and, for the larger whales, shape and size of the blow and how soon the dorsal fin appears relative to when you see the blow.

Breaching Humpback Whale

splash after breach

blow variable

pectoral flippers waving

fluke pattern highly variable

lumpy dorsal fin

blowholes

Humpback Whale (HUWH)

The staple of many whale-watching businesses. Fairly common off the Northeast May–Sep, migrating s. to breed in the Caribbean; found off the Southeast mainly in winter. Well-known for active displays at the surface, including tail- and flipper-slapping, breaching, and lunge-feeding. Often seen simply blowing, swimming, and diving (arching its back high but not fluking). With luck or patience, can be seen fluking before deeper dives. Blow bushy, but fairly high. Dorsal fin distinctive but variable, lumpy and fairly low; very long narrow flippers mostly white. Underside of tail varies from white to black; many individuals can be identified by tail pattern.

Fin (Finback) Whale (FIWH)

Fairly common off the Northeast spring–fall, with a few present in winter; ranges s. to Mid-Atlantic states in late fall–spring; very rarely seen s. of Cape Hatteras. Singly or in small groups; may associate with HUWH in rich feeding areas. Very large and often fast-swimming, with sloping fin typically wider at base than tall, slightly falcate (individually quite variable; cf. much smaller MIWH). Fin appears after blow and after a stretch of back rolls by. Blow taller and stronger than bushier blow of HUWH. Rarely flukes or breaches.

Lower jaw sides of Fin Whale differ in color: left side dark, right side white.

right lower jaw

Northern Minke Whale (MIWH)

The Minke (pronounced 'minky') is fairly common off New England spring–fall; very rarely seen to the s. Usually seen singly. Fast-swimming; resembles a mini FIWH but dorsal fin typically taller than wide, often more falcate. Blow low and bushy, usually not striking; fin appears simultaneously with blow, not after a length of back has appeared. Often rolls fairly high but rarely flukes, and after a few blows tends to disappear. Infrequent breaches can be clear out of the water.

Short flippers of Minke have a contrasting white band, visible with good views.

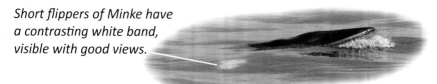

North Atlantic Right Whale (RIWH)

Total population only 500 or so animals. Rare to locally uncommon off the Northeast in spring–fall, mainly Apr–early May and late Sep–Nov. Moves s. to winter and calve off the Southeast, Dec–Mar. Found singly or in loose groups, mainly in nearshore waters. Blow bushy and, seen at the right angle, distinctly V-shaped. Large, blackish, and broad-bodied, without dorsal fin; flippers short and broad. Large head has variable whitish patches (callosities). Broad flukes often raised high when sounding.

sloping fin wide at base, appears after tall, strong blow

long back

falcate, shark-like fin appears at same time as weak blow

blowholes

lacks dorsal fin

V-shaped blow

massive head with strongly arched jawline

callosities

Sperm Whale (SPWH)

Uncommon in deeper offshore waters, usually just beyond the shelf break or over submarine canyons; singly or in loose groups. Off New England found mainly late summer–fall, but present year-round to the s. Bushy blow angled forward, not vertical. Dorsal fin low and triangular; massive head apparent at closer range; rear of body wrinkled. Rests at the surface (looks like a giant turd), blowing steadily before sounding for a deep dive, when usually shows its broad, triangular flukes. Feeds on squid in deep water, and dives can last 1–2 hours.

Pilot Whales (PIWH)

2 very similar species of large dolphins, smaller than true whales: **Long-finned Pilot Whale** and **Short-finned Pilot Whale** ('long' and 'short' refer to the pectoral flippers, rarely visible). Uncommon to fairly common in deep waters beyond the shelf break. Species identity usually presumed by location and temperature: Long-finned occurs in cooler waters off the Northeast, ranging s. to Mid-Atlantic states in winter; Short-finned in warmer waters off the Southeast, ranging n. to Mid-Atlantic states in summer–fall. Usually in groups of 5–50, often logging at the surface; rarely breach or show flukes. Blackish overall with blunt head. Dorsal fin low and wide-based, lobed at tip on adult male.

Beaked Whales occur in deep waters beyond the shelf break. Found as singles or small groups; often indifferent to boats but at times curious. Surfacing animals show beak first and then a low triangular dorsal fin (similar in all species), but do not fluke; rarely breach. Many sightings are noted simply as 'beaked whale sp.' (= species unidentified).

Cuvier's Beaked Whale (Goosebeak) (CUBW)

Uncommon from Mid-Atlantic states s., very rare n. to Cape Cod. Larger than dolphins, clearly smaller than typical whales. Low bushy blow inconspicuous. Color variable; adults have whitish head, and adult male is marked with whitish scratches. Surfacing animals often show distinctive short 'goosebeak' and roll fairly high, especially before sounding.

Mesoplodon Beaked Whales (MBWH)

The genus *Mesoplodon* contains numerous similar-looking species worldwide, all slightly smaller than CUBW; 4 occur off the East Coast but are seen infrequently. Usually surface and blow a few times before deep feeding dives. **Gervais's Beaked Whale** (GEBW) is regular off Cape Hatteras in spring–summer; status and distribution of other species not well known. Photos showing male teeth needed for species identification.

blow angled forward

low triangular dorsal fin

broad flukes

Short-finned

wide-based dorsal fin

presumed Short-finned

Long-finned

Cuvier's Beaked Whale

slightly falcate dorsal fin

male tooth at tip of beak

'goosebeak' face profile

Mesoplodon species

tooth along side of beak

beaked whales sp. (likely Gervais's)

Gervais's adult male

Risso's Dolphin (Grampus) (RIDO)

Uncommon to fairly common from Mid-Atlantic states s., mainly in deeper waters offshore from the shelf break; small numbers range n. to Gulf of Maine in summer–fall. This large dolphin is usually seen in small to fairly large groups, occasionally mixing with other species. Rarely bow-rides and often indifferent to boats; can be quite active but does not usually porpoise clear of the water; sometimes breaches. Note prominent, tall dorsal fin, blunt head, fairly large size. Dorsal fin shape variable, can resemble some BODO (below). Coloration also variable, from milky whitish to dark gray, typically with extensive scratch marks.

Bottlenose Dolphin (BODO)

Stereotypical, playful dolphin of aquariums and feel-good movies. Fairly common in warmer waters from Mid-Atlantic states southward, ranging n. in summer–fall to New England, where usually rare. 2 distinct populations: smaller inshore form ranges into coastal sounds and estuaries; larger offshore form occurs mainly beyond the shelf break. Singly or in groups of 2–10; offshore form at times in groups of 30 or more. Fairly large with prominent, falcate dorsal fin (cf. RIDO, above), stubby beak (often with white-tipped lower jaw), rather plain coloration. At times acrobatic, leaping high and tail-slapping, and offshore form often bow-rides; at other times simply swims by and is indifferent to boats.

immature Atlantic Spotted Dolphin lacks obvious spotting

Atlantic Spotted Dolphin (ASDO)

Uncommon to fairly common in warmer waters from Mid-Atlantic coast southward, mainly over the shelf (between the typical ranges of inshore and offshore BODO). Usually in groups of 5–20, rarely to 100 or more. Often bow-rides and is attracted to fast-moving boats; acrobatic, leaps and jumps readily. Fairly small, stocky dolphin with stout beak usually tipped white. Coloration highly variable: young are rather plain and unspotted, suggesting BODO but smaller, usually in company of spotted adults, and beak longer.

large, with blunt head, tall fin

thick, 'bottlenose' beak

Dolphins

Short-beaked Common Dolphin (SBCD)
Despite the name, not commonly seen on day trips off the East Coast. Can be found at Georges Bank (mainly spring–fall, when rare in Gulf of Maine), ranging s. (mainly winter–spring) to Mid-Atlantic states. Favors warmer waters from the shelf break to offshore. Inshore groups usually of 5–20 animals, but can occur in fast-moving, acrobatic groups of 100s. Handsome pattern easily seen as animals leap and bow-ride; note sharply demarcated creamy sides forward of dorsal fin.

fast-moving pod of Common Dolphins

Atlantic White-sided Dolphin (AWSD)
Fairly common off the Northeast; in winter–spring, very rare s. to Mid-Atlantic states. Usually in groups of 20–60, at times singles and small groups, rarely 100s; often in the same areas as feeding whales. Acrobatic, jumping and leaping, at times flipping head over tail. Sometimes bow-rides, but more often rather indifferent to boats. Note tall, falcate dorsal fin, short blunt beak; attractive 'white-sided' pattern best seen when animals leap.

Like all dolphins, Atlantic White-sided has variation in dorsal fin shape, but the upper individual looks like its fin was cut off, perhaps by a boat propeller.

Harbor Porpoise (HAPO)
Fairly common but often inconspicuous small porpoise of cooler inshore and island waters and tidal rips from New England northward; in winter ranges s. rarely to Mid-Atlantic Coast. Often seen from shore, rolling just beyond the breakers; rarely found far offshore. Usually singly or in groups of 3–10, at times larger groups in fall. Note low, triangular 'Hershey's Kiss' dorsal fin. Typically rolls once or twice before disappearing, but can swim quickly and create splashes. Rarely bow-rides.

*distinct beak,
striking side pattern*

*short blunt beak,
striking flank pattern*

inconspicuous, with low triangular dorsal fin

Rarer Whales and Dolphins (not to scale)

Sei Whale (SEWH)

The Sei (pronounced 'say') is a rather large, fast-swimming whale easily confused with much more numerous and larger Fin Whale and smaller Minke Whale (below and p. 14). Found occasionally off New England in spring–fall, mainly in deep offshore waters; exceptionally seen to the s. Differs from Fin in taller, more erect dorsal fin that appears just after the blow and is usually visible longer; both sides of lower jaw dark. Dorsal fin taller, more erect than Minke; lacks white flipper bands. Rarely rolls and doesn't fluke; usually sinks with dorsal fin tip the last thing to disappear.

Fin Whale

compare fin size and shape with Sei Whale

Minke Whale

Killer Whale (Orca) (KIWH)

This spectacular species, the largest dolphin, is rare off the Northeast (mainly summer–fall), very rare to the s. (mainly fall–winter). Unmistakable if seen well, but at a distance cf. Risso's Dolphin (p. 18). Blow puffy, not striking at a distance. Often first detected when fin of adult male towers out of the water. Females and younger males have smaller fins. Singly (mainly males) or in small groups, often moving quickly and can be difficult to keep track of; occasionally breaches.

False Killer Whale (FAKW)

This large dark dolphin is scarce in warm, deeper offshore waters of the Southeast; some move n. in summer–fall to Mid-Atlantic states. Usually in groups of 5–30, sometimes with other dolphins; at times bow-rides and curious around boats. Faster and more streamlined than Pilot Whales (p. 16), with distinctive, tall and blunt-topped dorsal fin. Often surfaces with blunt head clear of the water. Groups can be dispersed and very active, difficult to keep track of as they hunt fish; tail-slaps, leaps, and breaches.

False Killer fin tall, blunt-topped

Pilot Whale fin more sloping, broad-based

tall falcate fin appears just after blow

blowholes

female

adult male

blunt head

evenly blackish coloration

Kogias (Pygmy Sperm Whale, PYSW; Dwarf Sperm Whale, DWSW)

2 small, poorly known species (only 7–10 feet long), difficult to separate at sea and known collectively as kogias, for their genus name. Uncommon off the Southeast in warm deep waters beyond the shelf; Pygmy, at least, occurs rarely n. to New England in summer–fall. Very rarely seen unless seas are calm, typically as single animals logging at the surface. Wary of boats; usually dive with a low roll before you get close. As likely to be mistaken for a floating log as for any other marine mammal. Pygmy averages larger, with a slightly hump-backed profile forward of a lower, more sloping, and variably hooked dorsal fin; Dwarf has a flatter back and a taller, more prominent dorsal fin, but both species are variable.

Offshore Dolphins. In addition to the 2 species below, Pantropical Spotted Dolphin (very similar to Atlantic Spotted), Spinner Dolphin (similar to Clymene), and the handsome Striped Dolphin occur in the deep, warm offshore waters beyond the realm of day trips.

Rough-toothed Dolphin (RTDO)

Inhabits warm, deep Gulf Stream waters beyond the shelf break; found occasionally on day trips from Mid-Atlantic states south. Relatively unobtrusive and rarely bow-rides; very rarely leaps. Usually in groups of 10–20, often in tight swimming formation; typically rather slow-moving, but can move quickly at times. Note sloping triangular dorsal fin, rather 'reptilian' and sloping head with whitish to pale pink lips and lower jaw.

typical tight grouping of Rough-toothed Dolphins

Clymene Dolphin (Short-snouted Spinner) (CLDO)

The rather small Clymene Dolphin (pronounced Cly-me-nee) was not recognized as a full species until 1981, when it was separated from the highly variable Spinner Dolphin *Stenella longirostris*. It is scarce in warm, deep Gulf Stream waters beyond the shelf break, from Mid-Atlantic states south. Active and social, in groups of 5–50; bow-rides and leaps, at times head over tail while spinning. Note variable black 'lips' and distinct black tip to beak, sloping and slightly falcate dorsal fin. Spinner Dolphin has a longer and slimmer beak with black markings less distinct or absent.

Flotsam, such as above, can be mistaken easily for a kogia, and vice versa.

Kogia sp. (species unidentified)

sounding

Pygmy Sperm Whale

Dwarf Sperm Whale

Rough-toothed Dolphin

sloping dorsal fin

reptilian head, pale lips

Clymene Dolphin

black lips and beak tip

Seabirds

True seabirds live mainly beyond sight of shore, and include the tube-noses such as petrels and storm-petrels, and the alcids (diving birds including puffins, murres, and Dovekie). Many tubenoses are long-distance migrants that breed in the Southern Hemisphere; East Coast alcids are shorter-distance migrants that breed in the North Atlantic.

Gulls, often called 'seagulls,' are in fact mainly coastal birds, best seen and studied on shore. Especially in winter–spring, however, many gulls can be found offshore, such as over baitfish (below) or with Northern Gannets scavenging around fishing boats (opposite, below right). Only one gull in the East is a truly offshore species, rarely seen from land except during storms—the Black-legged Kittiwake (opposite, top right).

breeding adult has clean white head

immatures

non-breeding adults

solid black wing-tip

Black-legged Kittiwake (BLKI)

Fairly common to common Oct–Apr off Northeast; in smaller numbers Nov–Mar to Mid-Atlantic states; very rarely to FL; numbers vary year to year, sometimes a few stay into summer off the Northeast. Fairly small, long-winged gull. Adult has solid black wing-tip, plain yellow bill; immature has black M-pattern on upperwings. Breeds N Atlantic (and N Pacific).

Adult gulls are clean gray, black, and white; immatures are mottled brown and have black tail markings.

Shearwaters and Petrels

wings straighter than Cory's, wing-beats stiffer

dark morph (rare)

dark cap, black bill, smudgy underparts

light morph

large, stocky, superficially gull-like petrel with thick pale bill

Northern Fulmar (NOFU)

Mainly late fall–winter. Numbers vary year to year; usually scarce s. of New England. Bold scavenger, regularly follows boats, locally in 100s. Flies with wings held stiffly, but wingbeats often seem fluid. Breeds May–Sep in N Atlantic.

Great Shearwater (GRSH)

Common spring–fall in Northeast, variable numbers off Southeast (mainly Jun–Sep). Prefers cooler waters; often scavenges at fishing boats. Large flocks gather to molt, inshore to offshore. Breeds Nov–May in S Atlantic.

white 'fingers'

Scopoli's

variable white
flash on
coverts

grayish head,
big yellow bill,
clean underparts

dark body, narrow wings

Cory's Shearwater (COSH)

Common spring–fall off Southeast, fairly common summer–fall in Northeast. Prefers warmer waters. Flight more relaxed than GRSH. Mediterranean breeders ('Scopoli's Shearwater') average smaller, with more white on wing-tip. Breeds May–Oct in E Atlantic, winters S Atlantic.

Sooty Shearwater (SOSH)

Common summer–fall off Northeast, migrating in variable numbers off Southeast, mainly in spring. Can be seen from shore. Wingbeats deep and flight fast; wheels high in strong winds. Breeds Nov–Apr in Southern Hemisphere.

Shearwaters and Petrels

white stripes from molt

all plumages have big white rump patch

some birds have intermediate face patterns

dark-faced

white-faced types average narrower black underwing margins, weaker dark spur at sides of chest

white-faced

Black-capped Petrel (BCPE)

Uncommon to fairly common well offshore in warmer Gulf Stream waters from Cape Hatteras s.; very rare in fall n. to New England. Found singly or in loose aggregations; in calm, often rests on water with shearwaters, storm-petrels, etc. Flies with snappy wingbeats, buoyant wheeling glides. Distinctive: slightly smaller and stockier than Great Shearwater (p. 28), with big white rump patch, zippier flight. Many spring–summer birds are in obvious wing molt. Plumage variable: dark-faced and white-faced types may represent separate species. Breeds Dec–Jun in Caribbean.

Small Shearwaters. Two black-and-white species, found singly or in small groups. Much smaller than large shearwaters (pp. 28–29), with which they readily associate on the water and while feeding.

fall–winter wing molt

spring–summer wing molt

stockier than AUSH, with shorter tail, white undertail coverts.

relatively long tail, dark undertail coverts

white

dark

Manx Shearwater (MASH)

Fairly common spring–fall off Northeast, uncommon to rare year-round off Southeast. Prefers cooler waters than Audubon's Shearwater, often nearer shore. Flight strong and fast, banks high in strong winds. Breeds Apr–Sep in N Atlantic, most winter in S Atlantic.

Audubon's Shearwater (AUSH)

Fairly common spring–fall in warm Gulf Stream waters from Cape Hatteras s.; rare in summer–fall n. to New England; some winter off Florida. Flight usually low to the water; feeds while swimming in Sargassum mats. Breeds Jan–Jul in Bahamas and Caribbean.

Storm-Petrels

Very small seabirds, resembling bats or swallows that fly low over the water. Plumages similar; best identified by flight style, shape, relative size.

single Leach's among Wilson's

At rest on the water, Leach's and Band-rumped slightly larger and paler than Wilson's, with little or no white visible.

tail tip squared (rounded when spread)

long legs

toes project (difficult to see)

'walks on water' when feeding

Wilson's Storm-Petrel (WISP)

Common in spring–fall from Cape Hatteras n. to Gulf of Maine; smaller numbers off Southeast; can be seen from shore. Often follows boats and can gather in flocks of 100s at feeding slicks, pattering on the surface. Many spring–summer birds are in obvious wing molt. Swallow-like flight usually direct and fluttery. Breeds Dec–Apr in Antarctica.

Leach's and Band-rumped Storm-Petrels (opposite page) obviously larger and longer-winged in direct comparison, with deeper wingbeats, stronger and faster flight; usually seen singly or in small groups; do not stay around boats for long.

white wraps around

forked tail, long crooked wings

tail tip notched to squared

bold pale upperwing bands

narrow white rump band (cf. LHSP)

many spring–summer birds in wing molt

Leach's Storm-Petrel (LHSP)

Fairly common in spring–fall off Northeast, uncommon off Southeast, mainly well offshore. Typical flight strong and bounding, wings held crooked; flight in calm can be very like BRSP. Starts wing molt in summer–fall. Breeds May–Oct in N Atlantic, winters in Tropical Atlantic.

Band-rumped Storm-Petrel (BRSP)

Fairly common in spring–fall over warm, deep Gulf Stream waters off Southeast; rare in summer–fall n. to New England. Wing molt mainly in spring–summer, cf. LHSP. Flight typically less erratic than LHSP, with prolonged, shearing glides. Breeds Oct–Mar and Jun–Oct in E Atlantic.

Summer Alcids

Best seen on boat trips out to nesting islands in the Gulf of Maine. See winter birds on pp. 36–38.

adult with chick

<1% have white 'bridle'

Common Murre (COMU)

Fairly common breeder locally in Gulf of Maine, May–Aug. Inshore to offshore, locally in 100s; cf. RAZO. In summer–fall, male travels with chick (male gives guttural growls, chick has far-carrying reedy whistles). See winter birds on p. 36.

Razorbill (RAZO)

Uncommon breeder locally in Gulf of Maine, May–Aug. Often associates with more numerous Common Murre. Stockier and blacker than murre, with distinctive bill shape and pattern, longer tail. See winter birds on p. 37.

juvenile (Aug–Oct)

Atlantic Puffin (ATPU)

Uncommon breeder locally in Gulf of Maine, May–Aug. Mainly offshore, singly or in small groups. Unmistakable if seen well, with 'clown face' and fancy bill. See winter birds on p. 38.

Black Guillemot (BLGU)

Fairly common breeder locally in Gulf of Maine, May–Aug. Often seen from shore, usually as singles or small groups. Breeding plumage striking; juvenile dingy overall with messy dark markings, cf. larger COMU. See winter birds on p. 37.

Larger Winter Alcids

Unless seas are calm it can be very difficult to spot alcids on the water. They are usually shy of moving boats, and quickly dive to escape or run along the surface to take off and fly straight away. See pp. 34–35 for summer birds, p. 38 for winter puffin and Dovekie.

molting birds darker-faced

bulkier than Common, blacker above

white gape line diagnostic but often hard to see

white face with dark eyestripe

dark head with whitish chin

Common Murre (COMU)

Uncommon to fairly common s. to Mid-Atlantic Coast (mainly Nov–Mar). Singly or in small numbers, associating readily with RAZO and TBMU.

Thick-billed Murre (TBMU)

Uncommon to rare (numbers vary year to year) s. to Mid-Atlantic Coast (mainly Nov–Mar). Singly or in small numbers, associating readily with RAZO and COMU. Breeds N Atlantic, n. of US.

snowy Arctic types seen
rarely in Northeast

adults

adult

immature lacks
white bill stripes
of adult

immature's white
wing panels
smaller than adult

dark 'helmet' with thick bill

'white-headed' with small bill

Razorbill (RAZO)

Fairly common to locally common
s. to Mid-Atlantic Coast (mainly
Nov–Mar), rarely to the Southeast.
Often nearer shore than murres,
over shoals and banks, where can
occur in flocks, locally of 100s.

Black Guillemot (BLGU)

Fairly common in the Northeast,
mainly on nearshore waters and
often seen from land; very rare
(mainly Dec–Feb) s. to Mid-Atlantic
states. Singly or in small flocks, usually separate from other alcids.

Smaller Winter Alcids

These 2 sought-after species are smaller than the other alcids (pp. 36–37) and have dark underwings that contrast in flight with their white bodies. Puffins are usually found as singles well offshore; Dovekies can occur in flocks and sometimes are seen from shore, even in harbors.

dirty pale face, dark underwings

clean black-and-white pattern, dark underwings

immature has smaller bill than adult

fairly small and chunky, with dirty pale face, deep bill

very small and stocky, like a mini murre or Razorbill with a stubby bill

Atlantic Puffin (ATPU)

Uncommon to rare s. to Mid-Atlantic states (mainly Nov–Apr). Usually well offshore at fronts and near the shelf break. Typically seen singly, separate from other alcids; flight fast and usually low over the water.

Dovekie (DOVE)

Notably erratic in occurrence, this 'bathtub-toy alcid' is scarce in some years, common in others, s. to Mid-Atlantic states (mainly Nov–Mar). Singly or in groups, usually not with other alcids. Breeds in High Arctic.

Small sandpipers that swim. Breed on Arctic tundra and winter at sea. Often in flocks along current edges and on glassy strips of water; the 2 species readily associate together.

breeding plumage

immature/non-breeding plumage

plain, pale gray back

variable back striping

molting adults

relatively large and bulky; bill thicker than RNPH and pale-based

Red Phalarope (REPH)

Fairly common (Apr–May, Sep–Nov) off Northeast, uncommon off Mid-Atlantic states and Southeast. In winter, uncommon off Southeast, rare n. to Cape Cod. Call a high tinny *tink*, distinct from lower-pitched, clipped *tik* of RNPH.

Red-necked Phalarope (RNPH)

Fairly common (May, Aug–Sep) off Northeast, less common s. to Mid-Atlantic states; uncommon in Southeast. Note very fine black bill; in fall, often looks black-and-white overall. Winters s. of US.

white eyebrow

whitish

breeding plumage adults

dark hindneck in all plumages (whitish on Bridled)

immatures

immature Sooty has dark head and body

dark

white

broader-winged and more buoyant than Bridled

immature/non-breeding plumage often looks white-headed

Sooty Tern (SOTE)

Fairly common spring–fall off FL, uncommon to fairly common n. in summer–fall to Mid-Atlantic states. Very rarely perches on flotsam; often in flocks of 5–50 birds over feeding groups of shearwaters, etc. Sails and soars high, unlike BRTE. Breeds Tropical Atlantic.

Bridled Tern (BRTE)

Uncommon to fairly common spring–fall in Gulf Stream waters n. to Mid-Atlantic states; a few range n. to New England in summer–fall. Often perches on flotsam; usually seen singly or in 2s and 3s, often along weedlines. Breeds in Caribbean.

narrower black than Common

contrast

translucent

immatures

distinct blackish

whitish (dark on Common)

breeding plumage adults

uniform, no contrast

contrast

short head/neck/bill, long narrow wings with translucent primaries

longer head/neck/bill than Arctic, primaries not translucent

Arctic Tern (ARTE)

Uncommon migrant offshore, May–Jun and Aug–Sep; breeds locally in n. Gulf of Maine. Singly or in small flocks; at times rests on flotsam. Many small 'white terns' are not easily identified given typical views, best called Common/Arctic. Winters around Antarctica.

Common Tern (COTE)

Fairly common to common migrant inshore to offshore, Apr–May and Jul–Oct; breeds from Gulf of Maine s. to Mid-Atlantic states. Singly or flocks, at times in 100s; mixes readily with other terns. Smoother, less clipped wingbeats than Arctic Tern. Winters s. of US.

Jaegers

Jaegers (pronounced 'yay-gers') resemble dark, streamlined gulls; all 3 species have white wing flashes. Plumage highly variable, especially immatures; often difficult to identify to species. Pomarine and Parasitic adults have a dark morph. Breed on Arctic tundra and spend non-breeding periods at sea. Feed by pirating other seabirds, forcing them to regurgitate their food.

breeding plumage adults

dark morph

'spoon-tipped'

subadult

winter adult

immatures

subadults

Pomarine Jaeger (POJA)

Largest jaeger; fairly common spring and fall, uncommon in winter off Southeast. All ages have thick, blunt-tipped tail projections (long and 'spoon-tipped' on adults); also note relatively big bill, broad wings. As on other jaegers, underwing barred on immature, solidly dark on adult. Often in wing molt in fall. Often follows boats, associates on water with shearwater flocks; chases gulls and shearwaters.

breeding plumage adults

sharp point

often broken or shed in fall

dark morph

subadult

strong contrast

immatures

crescent of white shafts

2 white shafts

Parasitic Jaeger (PAJA)

Medium-size; fairly common spring and fall, scarce in winter off Southeast; nearer shore than other jaegers. Angular and falcon-like, with pointed tail projections. Immature often warm-toned (some all-dark). Chases terns and smaller gulls.

Long-tailed Jaeger (LTJA)

Smallest jaeger; uncommon to rare in spring and fall; winters s. of US. Graceful, with long slender tail, 2–3 white shafts on upperwing. Immature cold-toned (some all-dark). Chases terns, gulls, storm-petrels.

Skuas

Usually seen singly; scavenge, and pirate gulls and shearwaters.

fall–winter wing molt

spring–fall wing molt

adults

head and body pale to dark brown

adults

warm-toned; adult has variable rusty and buff mottling on upperparts; immature plainer and darker

cold-toned; lacks coarse pale mottling of adult GRSK

Great Skua (GRSK)

Scarce in Gulf of Maine May–Oct; from New England s. to Mid-Atlantic states Nov–Mar. Usually wary of boats, rarely seen up close. Mainly found in areas with gulls, gannets, large shearwaters, etc. Breeds May–Sep in NE Atlantic.

South Polar Skua (SPSK)

Scarce off Northeast Jun–Oct, off Southeast May–Jun. Some birds quite tame, scavenging boldly at boats; others simply fly past. Mainly chases large shearwaters, gulls. Cf. dark Pomarine Jaeger (p. 42). Breeds Nov–Mar in Antarctica.

Spectacular seabirds, usually seen as 1s and 2s; often attracted to boats.

broad white tips (narrow on RBTR)

big black patches
diagnostic

adults

orange
bill

adults and subadults have
long white tail streamers

red bill

white

black wedge

immatures

immatures of both species have short, black-tipped tails,
finely barred backs, yellowish bills

adult

White-tailed Tropicbird (WTTR)

Scarce off Southeast in spring–fall, very rarely to Northeast in summer–fall. Mostly adults and subadults seen; a few immatures occur in fall. All plumages have white primary coverts, cf. RBTR. Breeds Bermuda and Caribbean.

Red-billed Tropicbird (RBTR)

Scarce in spring–fall off Southeast, very rare in Northeast; immatures occur spring–fall. Slightly bulkier than WTTR, with black primary coverts on upperwing; all plumages barred above; immature has yellow bill, cf. WTTR. Breeds Caribbean.

Gannet and Boobies
Very large, streamlined diving birds

dark, unlike MABO

immatures

*immature gannets
highly variable*

extensive white

white collar

1st-years

yellowish

adults

pointed gape

dark mask, yellowish bill

subadults

Northern Gannet (NOGA)

Common in n. Gulf of Maine spring–fall; in winter (mainly Nov–Mar), common from New England s. to Mid-Atlantic states; smaller numbers s. to FL. Often seen from shore. 1st-year brown overall; like adult in 3 years. Breeds N Atlantic.

Masked Booby (MABO)

Scarce in spring–fall off Southeast, usually well offshore in warm waters. Mostly seen singly; may check out boats. Smaller, more lightly built than NOGA. 1st-year brown-and-white; like adult in 2–3 years. Breeds Tropical Atlantic.

Very large, angular, and aerial

adult

*clean-cut
brown/white
divide*

1st-years

*adult male black;
red throat balloon
inflates in display*

*1st-year brownish below;
like adult in 2–3 years*

*immature has white
head and chest; like
adult in 6+ years*

*adult female
(male bill greenish)*

*adult female has
black head, white chest*

all plumages solidly brown above

Brown Booby (BRBO)

Uncommon spring–fall off FL, rare n. in summer–fall to Mid-Atlantic states, exceptionally New England. Inshore to offshore; can be seen from land. Slightly smaller, more lightly built than MABO. Breeds Tropical Atlantic.

Magnificent Frigatebird (MAFR)

Scarce off cen. FL; in summer–fall, rare n. to Mid-Atlantic states. More often along coast than offshore. Unmistakable. Flight buoyant, sails easily on arched wings; does not alight on water. Pirates terns and boobies. Breeds Tropical Atlantic.

Gadfly Petrels. Petrels in the genus *Pterodroma* are known as gadfly petrels, for their impetuous arcing flight in high winds. They favor warm, deep, offshore waters beyond the continental shelf. Only off Cape Hatteras is it routine to see gadflies on a day trip: Black-capped Petrel (p. 30) is regular, and 2 smaller species (Trinidade and Fea's) are rare visitors.

underparts highly variable

contrasting dark underwings

paler tail

palest on primaries (cf. SOSH, p. 29)

clean white

variable white panels

Trinidade (Herald) Petrel (TRPE)

Rare in spring–fall, mainly May–Sep off Cape Hatteras. Flight fast and buoyant, quicker and more graceful than shearwaters. Plumage variable, some dark-bodied (cf. SOSH, p. 29); all types dark brown above. Breeds Oct–Mar in S Atlantic.

Fea's Petrel (FEPE)

Rare in spring–fall, mainly May–Jun off Cape Hatteras. Flight fast and buoyant, sailing and wheeling easily even in light winds. Gray upperparts blend against sea, but underparts striking. Breeds year-round in E Atlantic.

Sabine's Gull (SAGU)

Rare offshore migrant, Aug–Oct; very rare late spring. Small, distinctive, elegant gull with bright white triangles on upperwing, tern-like flight. Breeds on Arctic tundra, migrates through E Atlantic to winter off Africa.

White-faced Storm-Petrel (WFSP)

Scarce fall visitor (late Jul–early Oct) off New England and Mid-Atlantic states. Singly, or loosely in 2s and 3s; not usually with other species. Flies low over the sea, often splash-kicking with its feet, swerving and gliding erratically; easily lost against the water. Breeds Jan–Sep in E Atlantic.

Sea Turtles

Sea Turtles are large marine reptiles found worldwide in warmer waters. 3 species are seen regularly off the East Coast; 2 other species (Kemp's Ridley and Hawksbill Turtle) are very rare and not covered here.

Views of turtles at sea are usually brief, often simply the head of an animal basking at the surface before it dives at the approach of a boat. For species identification, try to get a photo of the head or back from above; still, many sightings are best logged as turtle sp. (= species unidentified). Beware: While active turtles need to surface every few minutes, resting animals can remain underwater for a few hours!

Sea turtles go to sea as tiny hatchlings mostly at the mercy of sea currents; after a few years they reach the size of a dinner plate and are able to swim for themselves, but still require 10–30 years to develop into mature adults. Adult females come ashore to lay eggs every 1–4 years, but after hatching the males may never come ashore. As with many marine animals, some species make long migrations between feeding areas and breeding areas.

Black Terns Chlidonias niger *resting on a Loggerhead Turtle.*

Leatherback Turtle *Dermochelys coriacea*. Uncommon but widespread, adults and subadults range northward in summer–fall; often occurs in cooler waters than other turtles. Distinctive, the largest turtle (adult length averages 6–7 feet). Note smooth leathery back with 5 distinct ridges, large head. Dark overall, often with paler blotches and spots.

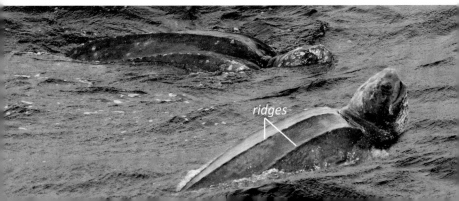

ridges

Loggerhead Turtle *Caretta caretta*. Most frequently seen sea turtle off East Coast; adult shell length averages 3–4 feet. Occurs year-round off the Southeast, ranging n. to New England in summer–fall. Note overall orange to reddish-brown coloration (can be obscured on shell by greenish mottling, but flippers usually orange to brownish); large broad head with short beak. With good views, note 5 plates along side of shell, 4 or more small plates between eyes. Cf. immature Green Turtle (radial streaked pattern to orange plates; olive flippers; 2 large plates between eyes).

barnacles on shell

typically orange-brown overall

short blunt beak

radial streaks

Loggerhead

4+ smaller plates between eyes

2 larger plates between eyes

Green

immature Green

no beak

Green Turtle *Cheldonia mydas*. Generic, 'gentle-faced' sea turtle of children's books; adult shell length averages 3–4 feet. Adults uncommon or rare off East Coast, mainly inshore in FL. Immatures commoner, ranging n. to New England, mainly in summer–fall. Adult shell grayish or brownish overall with variable patterning, head blunt with rounded face and no distinct beak (sides of head have contrasting, creamy-edged blackish plates). Immature very different in color, bright orange-brown with radial streaked pattern on shell plates; cf. Loggerhead. With good view, note 4 plates along side of shell and 2 relatively large, long plates between eyes.

Flyingfish

The seas are home to many fish, but most are not easily viewed from a boat. An exception is **flyingfish**, which number 60 or so species worldwide in waters usually warmer than 70°F. About 10 species occur year-round off the Southeast, and in summer–fall some range to the Northeast. Most have 2 pairs of 'wings,' the forewings (pectoral fins) always larger than the hindwings (pelvic fins); the lower tail lobe is longer than the upper.

Usually 6–14 inches long with 'wingspans' up to 2 feet, flyingfish shoot out of the water and glide away from approaching boats, as if escaping from a predator (which is why they fly). Some species are seen as singles, whereas small species often occur in groups, at times of 100s.

Matching images to formal scientific names is often not possible, but several types can be identified. The commoner types are shown here (genus or presumed species names are given in parentheses).

dorsal fin

Small (about 6–10 inches across); wings plain or clear; often in groups

lacks hindwings

Oddspot Midget (*Parexocoetus hillianus?*). Black spot on big dorsal fin, which flips to either side like a 5th wing. Fairly common.

Small Clearwing (*Exocoetus*). 2 wings (small pelvic fins cloaked by big forewings); uncommon to fairly common, offshore.

pink blush created by veins

purplish band

variable dark marks

Rosy-veined Clearwing (*Cypselurus comatus?*). 4 wings, medium-size; uncommon, usually singles.

Purple Bandwing. 4 wings, small; fairly common, singles or small groups. Probably immature stages of patchwing and/or necromancer.

variable dusky forewing patches, can be tinged pinkish

forewings
(pectoral fins)

Atlantic Patchwing
(Cheilopogon melanurus?
Hirundichthys affinis?)

hindwings
(pelvic fins)

dark in tail

Larger, 4–wing flyingfish, usually seen singly or in small groups, include **Atlantic Patchwing**, often the commonest type off Hatteras, and 3 less numerous, dark-winged types: **Midnightwing**, **Atlantic Necromancer**, and **Double Midnight**. These can fly hundreds of yards.

black with white margin

paler band

plain

contrasting black

Midnightwing
(Cheilopogon cyanopterus?)

Atlantic Necromancer
(Cheilopogon exsiliensis?)

Double Midnight
(Hirundichthys rondeletii?)

blue-black

big black patches

The tail of a flyingfish acts like a propeller (right) and can kick a zig-zag wake in the surface to power extra flights.

Flyingfish and Flying Squid

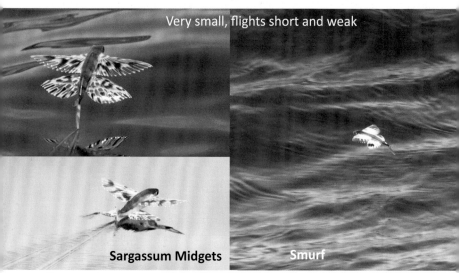

Very small, flights short and weak

Sargassum Midgets

Smurf

Small, ornately patterned flyingfish such as **Sargassum Midgets** (also known as 'grasshoppers' because they frequent weedlines, or grasslines) are about 2–3 inches across. These are cryptically patterned juveniles, which grow up to look very different as adults. **Smurfs** are very young juveniles, about an inch across; often they look like tiny bubbles blowing in the wind.

As if flyingfish weren't enough, **flying squid** can be seen on occasion, mainly in deep offshore waters and singly or in groups upwards of 50. They usually make single, fairly short flights (powered by pulsing jets of water) and then disappear, leaving you to wonder whether you really saw them! Most are less than 6 inches long.

flattened tentacles

Other Fish

Unless the ocean is calm you are unlikely to see many fish from a boat, although sometimes small baitfish 'boil' at the surface when pursued from below by larger fish (photo p. 26). On calm sunny days with clear water, however, it is possible to see a variety of fish species (too many to cover here), especially off the Southeast under flotsam or in weed patches. Among the more frequently seen species are the stunning **Dolphinfish** *Coryphaena hippurus* (a popular target of sport fishermen) and the somberly mottled **Atlantic Tripletail** *Lobotes surinamensis*, which often lies sluggishly near the surface. And then you might just see some oddball, like the bizarre **Porcupinefish** *Diodon hystrix*.

Dolphinfish (Mahi-mahi)
(up to 6.5 feet long)

vivid turquoise, green, and yellow coloration fades soon after death

Atlantic Tripletail (up to 3.5 feet long)

Porcupinefish (up to 2.5 feet long)

spines erected

Billfish and Sharks

Large but infrequently seen, billfish and sharks are evocative oceanic inhabitants, the former much sought after by sport fishermen.

Billfish. Most views of billfish are of briefly seen dorsal and tail fins, sometimes thrashing to ball bait at the surface, but on occasion Sailfish can leap clear of the water.

Sailfish *Istiophorus platypterus* (to 11 feet) occurs from FL n. to Mid-Atlantic states. **Blue Marlin** *Makaira nigricans* (to 14.5 feet) and **White Marlin** *Kajikia albida* (to 9 feet) occur off the entire East Coast, in warmer waters.

dorsal 'sail' flattened when leaping

pelvic fins shorter than on marlins

White Marlin

dorsal fin tip rounded (pointed on Blue Marlin)

Sailfish

dorsal fin large, sail-like, and jagged-edged

Sharks are seen occasionally on pelagic trips, and some 50 species occur off the East Coast. Many are not readily identified in the field, given that all you usually get is a brief view of a dorsal fin and sometimes the tail fin—a bit of an anticlimax if you are hoping for a *Jaws*-type encounter. Beware: the fins of Molas (p. 58) can be mistaken for sharks.

tail (caudal fin)

dorsal fin

*The very broad-based, triangular dorsal fin of **Basking Shark** (above and opposite page) is fairly distinctive, especially given the animal's large size. The tall, narrow, blunt-tipped dorsal fin of a **hammerhead shark** (right) is also fairly distinctive.*

Among the more frequently seen sharks are **hammerhead sharks** (genus *Sphyrna*, 4 species; up to 19 feet long) in warmer waters off the Southeast; the impressive **Basking Shark** *Cetorhinus maximus* (up to 32 feet), off the Northeast in spring–fall, ranging s. to Mid-Atlantic states in winter; and the sleek **Blue Shark** *Prionace glauca* (up to 12 feet) off the Northeast, mainly in spring–fall.

hammerhead 'horns'

In clear water, the distinctive, eponymous head of a hammerhead shark can sometimes be seen.

The massive **Basking Shark** is nonaggressive and feeds sluggishly on plankton near the surface.

In good light, the slender **Blue Shark** can appear quite blue, but more often (as with most sharks) you see just the fins.

Other Big Fish

Ocean Sunfish (Mola) *Mola mola*. One fish that is seen fairly often from boats is the bizarre Ocean Sunfish, or Mola, which often occurs near the surface, singly or in loose groups. Found year-round off the Southeast, it ranges n. to New England in summer–fall. Molas are laterally compressed and often lie on their side, looking like a trashcan lid and loosely waving a shark-like fin above the surface. Most Molas are 2–6 feet across, but the largest can be more than 10 feet across and weigh over 2 tons.

Groups of Molas usually involve smaller animals; the bigger individuals typically occur singly.

Lying on its side, a Mola often looks ghostly whitish, and its dorsal fin (left) can be mistaken easily for that of a shark.

Rays *are seen occasionally in warm shelf waters off the Southeast, usually as dark 'flying carpets' just below the surface, but sometimes breaching like this* **devil ray** *(genus Mobula), which can reach 4 feet across.*

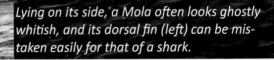

Giant Manta Ray *Manta birostris* is the largest ray (reaching 23 feet across) and occurs year-round off the Southeast; in summer it ranges n. rarely to New England. As on devil rays (opposite, bottom), two 'head fins' create flexible 'horns' either side of the mouth. Manta can be told from the much smaller devil rays by its huge size and relatively short tail.

'wing-tips' sometimes break the surface

Whale Shark *Rhincodon typus*. With its huge size (up to 40 feet long, but most are 20–30 feet) and white polka-dot pattern, this largest of all fish is readily identifiable. A placid filter-feeder, it occurs in warmer waters off the Southeast, rarely ranging n. to New England in summer–fall. Seeing one on a pelagic trip is a rare treat, but you might get lucky...

nostrils

When vacuuming up plankton, only the wide mouth may show above water, as in the head-on view above.

dorsal fin is broad-based, rounded, and variably spotted

tail *dorsal fin* *mouth*

Seaweeds

Most **seaweeds** (also known as algae) grow attached to something, but the golden **Sargassum** weeds (or gulfweeds) have a pelagic lifestyle. They drift along in the Gulf Stream, often bunching up in big patches at fronts (see p. 6). There are 2 fully pelagic species: *Sargassum natans* and *S. fluitans*; *natans* has narrower fronds and 'nipples' on its float bladders; *fluitans* has wider fronds and smooth, berry-like float bladders.

Sargassum natans   *S. fluitans*

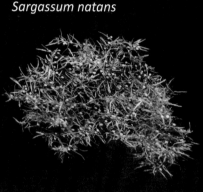

Not all examples are as clearly different as these, and mats often contain the 2 species tangled together.

As well as being important egg-laying substrates and nurseries for many fish species, *Sargassum* mats host a remarkable assemblage of life forms adapted to live amid the miniature forest of fronds. If you scoop up some weed in a bucket and look carefully, you can find many types of sea life, such as the juvenile filefish shown below.

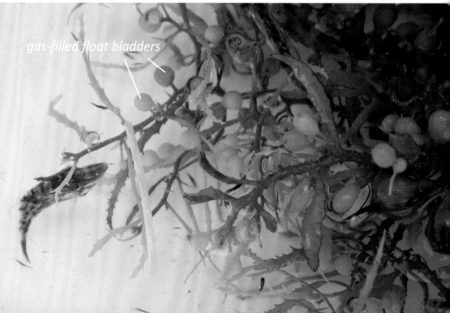

gas-filled float bladders

By-the-wind Sailor (Velella) *Velella velella*. Some years, mainly spring–fall in warmer waters, countless 1000s of this free-floating hydrozoan (a jellyfish cousin) can dot the sea suface, at times blown into silvery bands at fronts and washing ashore on beaches. Each Velella measures 2–4 inches across, with a rubbery blue mantle and a stiff silvery sail—its only means of locomotion.

Portuguese Man O'War *Physalia physalia*. Famous for its long stinging tentacles, this wind-drifted hydrozoan can be fairly common in Gulf Stream waters off the Southeast, ranging to the Northeast in summer–fall. The balloon-like float-sail is usually 4–8 inches across and varies in color from silvery to vivid purple. Mainly seen singly, at times a few together at fronts.

At a distance can look like a small plastic bag.

Blown on its side, tentacles are more easily visible.

tentacles

Jellyfish and Cousins

Jellyfish. On some trips you may see 100s, even 1000s of jellyfish, but on many trips none are seen. Often they are commonest inshore and along fronts such as the Gulf Stream edge. Among the most frequent species are the ghostly, frisbee-size **moon jellies** (genus *Aurelia*) and grapefruit-size **Cannonball Jellyfish** *Stomolophus meleagris*, both of which can be common off the Southeast in summer–fall. The **Lion's Mane Jellyfish** *Cyanea capillata*, found in cooler waters from Maine s. to Mid-Atlantic states, is the largest known jelly: most are 1–3 feet across, but they can be 7 feet, with tentacles 120 feet long!

Moon Jelly

Cannonball Jelly

Lion's Mane Jelly 'sheltering' lots of tiny fish.

Landbirds. But wait, isn't this book about offshore wildlife? Sure enough, but every year millions of landbirds migrate and many of them fly over water, some intentionally, others not. Especially in fall you may see landbirds far out at sea, as well as migrating herons, ducks, shorebirds, even raptors. Exhausted birds often land on boats, sometimes even on people!

This fall flock of warblers was 50 miles off the coast of Florida, headed to the Bahamas or points south.

Mammals

ASDO Atlantic Spotted Dolphin *Stenella frontalis* 10, 18–19
AWSD Atlantic White-sided Dolphin *Lagenorhynchus acutus* 20–21
BODO Common Bottlenose Dolphin *Tursiops truncatus* 18–19
CLDO Clymene Dolphin *Stenella clymene* 24–25
CUBW Cuvier's Beaked Whale *Ziphius cavirostris* 16–17
DWSW Dwarf Sperm Whale *Kogia simus* 24–25
FAKW False Killer Whale *Pseudorca crassidens* 9, 22–23
FIWH Fin Whale *Balaenoptera physalus* 14–15, 22
GEBW Gervais's Beaked Whale *Mesoplodon europaeus* 16–17
HAPO Harbor Porpoise *Phocoena phocoena* 20–21
HUWH Humpback Whale *Megaptera novaeangliae* 10, 12–13
KIWH Killer Whale (Orca) *Orcinus orca* 22–23
MIWH Northern Minke Whale *Balaenoptera acutorostrata* 14–15, 22
PIWH Pilot Whales (Short-finned *Globiocephala macrorhynchus*;
          Long-finned *Globiocephala melas*) 16–17, 22
PYSW Pygmy Sperm Whale *Kogia breviceps* 24–25
RIDO Risso's Dolphin *Grampus griseus* 18–19
RIWH North Atlantic Right Whale *Eubalaena glacialis* 14–15
RTDO Rough-toothed Dolphin *Steno bredanensis* 24–25
SBCD Short-beaked Common Dolphin *Delphinus delphis* 20–21
SEWH Sei Whale *Balaenoptera borealis* 22–23
SPWH Sperm Whale *Physeter macrocephalus* 16–17

Birds

ARTE Arctic Tern *Sterna paradisaea* 41
ATPU Atlantic Puffin *Fratercula arctica* 35, 38
AUSH Audubon's Shearwater *Puffinus lherminieri* 31
BCPE Black-capped Petrel *Pterodroma hasitata* 30
BLGU Black Guillemot *Cepphus grylle* 35, 37
BLKI Black-legged Kittiwake *Rissa tridactyla* 27
BRBO Brown Booby *Sula leucogaster* 47
BRSP Band-rumped Storm-Petrel *Oceanodroma castro* 33
BRTE Bridled Tern *Onychoprion anaethetus* 40
COMU Common Murre *Uria aalge* 34, 36
COSH Cory's Shearwater *Calonectris [diomedea] borealis* 29
COTE Common Tern *Sterna hirundo* 41
DOVE Dovekie *Alle alle* 7, 38
FEPE Fea's Petrel *Pterodroma feae* 48
GRSH Great Shearwater *Ardenna gravis* 28
GRSK Great Skua *Catharacta skua* 44
LHSP Leach's Storm-Petrel *Oceanodroma leucorhoa* 32, 33

Species Codes, Scientific Names, and Index (cont.)

The East Coast (opposite). Dark blue dots show selected ports from which whale-watching and pelagic birding trips originate. To find out about trips, simply Google, for example, 'Massachusetts whale-watching trips' or 'Ponce de Leon, Florida, pelagic trips' and that should lead you to a list of operators, trips, and dates. As you can see, most are clustered from Maine to Cape Cod. Trips off the Southeast, south of Hatteras, North Carolina, tend to be few and far between.